Rotten Pumpkin

By David M. Schwartz
Photos by Dwight Kuhn

Creston Books

A Rotten Tale in 15 Voices

Here I stand, bright with light, proud and round.
Tonight is my glory night. Call me Jack.

My flame is spent. No more do I glow. Back to the garden I go.

Some think mice like me are cute nibbling on a pumpkin, but it's not cute being everybody else's lunch. Weasel, gopher, owl, snake, badger, bobcat, house cat, rat — they all want mouse pie! I'm always on the lookout for danger cuz danger's on the lookout for me.

Squirrels are nutty about nuts and flaky about fruit, but I've just had my fill, so no pump-kin right now, thank you. Oh, I see a seed, so I'll grab it and head for my favorite tree.

Call me slug, the eating machine. I scrape food into my mouth with my sharp little tongue. Look closely and you'll see marks on the pumpkin. Like footprints, they show you where I've been and they make great spots for mold spores to touch down and grow. I hope those molds appreciate what I do for them!

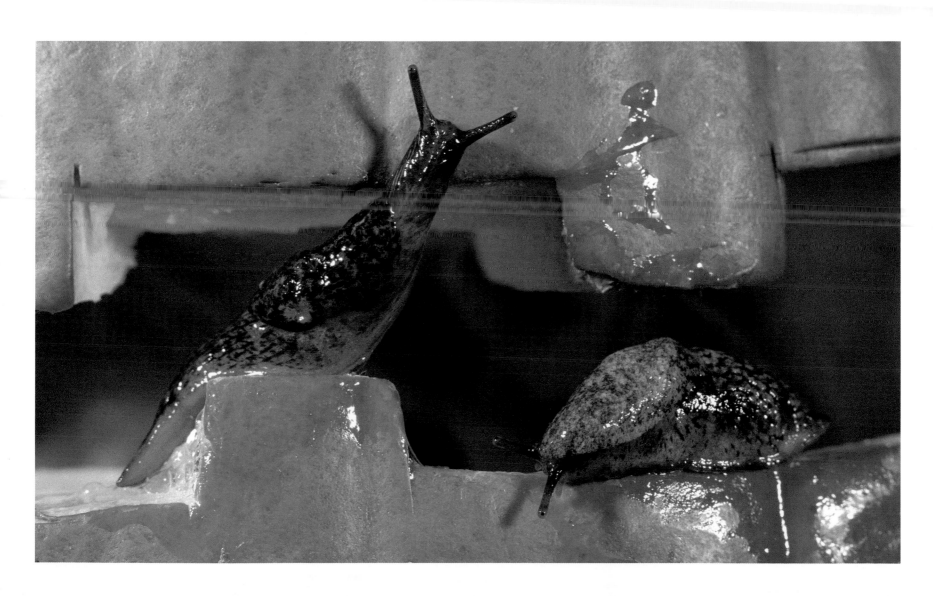

My keen fly nose smells what I am looking for — dead fish, rotten meat, dog doo — the stinkier, the better! A rotting pumpkin is perfect. I taste it with my feet. You're gonna love hearing how I eat. I vomit on the pumpkin flesh. My vomit dissolves pumpkin nutrients so I can lap them up. A delicious, nutritious morning smoothie!

My big night is just a memory.
My smile has faded, my crown
is down. Where once I smiled
and winked, now fungi ring
my mouth and eyes. A cheerful
Jack I am no more.

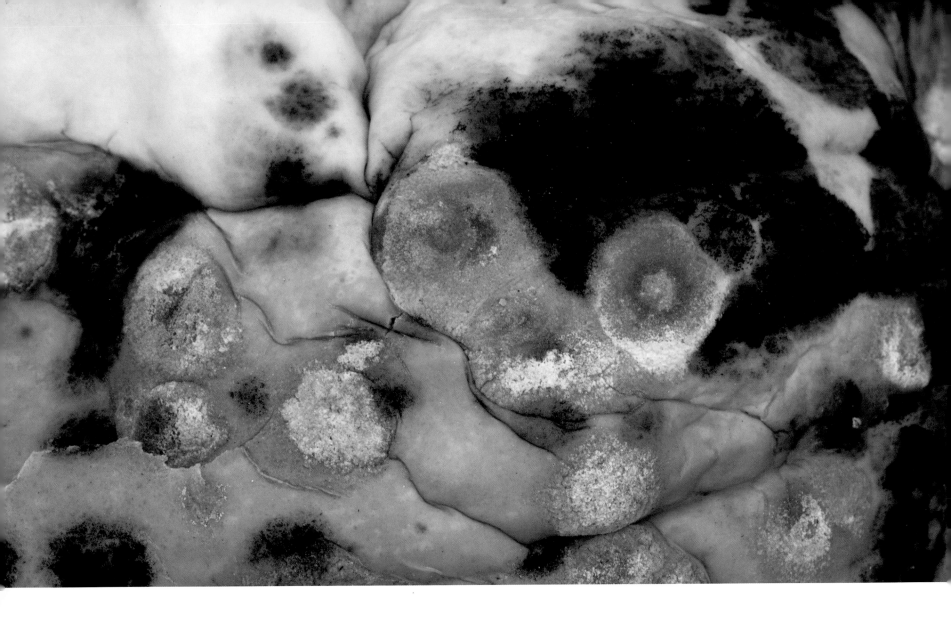

I'm a mold with a nasty name. People call me "black rot." I'm black and I rot! Someone cut holes into this pumpkin and that really helped me out. Now I've got soft, fresh pumpkin flesh for lunch. Rotten fellow that I am, I'll turn Jack to mush.

Black rot, I appreciate you. I'm Fusarium rot, and you prepared the pumpkin's skin for me like a gardener's hoe prepares the earth. I landed as a spore and from tiny gray spores great reddish fungi can grow. Now you're gone, but I'm living off the "land" you readied for me—pumpkin land.

Have you ever noticed a slice of bread dotted with gray blotches? A strawberry growing white fuzz? A pumpkin wearing earmuffs? Then you've seen me! I'm sometimes called "bread mold" but I've got an appetite for a lot more than bread. Once my spores land on something yummy, I grow fast-fast-fast. Then I send up tiny pinheads filled with more spores, like teeny, tiny seeds. Into the air they go. If they land on another pumpkin, they'll give it earmuffs and a new nose.

Hear this, all you molds and rots: I, the sow bug, owe you! Without you, I'd be under a log, chewing rotten wood. My mouthparts can't break through a pumpkin's skin, but you softened it up so now I can munch its deliciously rotten flesh. I'll repay you by getting you to your next pumpkin. I'm sure to swallow bits of mold and when I poop, I'll leave it behind. In other words, I'll spread you around. So I can thank you, and you can thank me. We're even.

I may be one scary-looking dude, but I'm the one who's scared. I've got a bad case of mold – three, four, maybe five or more of them, and look what they're doing to me!

But see the clean spot below my lower lip on the right side? I'll tell you why I look so good there. First look a little further up and to the right. See that fuzzy grayish greenish area? That's not just any old mold.

I am the famous Penicillium.

The drug Penicillin is made from me and has saved millions of human lives.

Let me explain. Naturally, I'd rather not share my food with other molds or bacteria. When they start growing too close, I make chemicals that kill them off. See how the lower lip of this pumpkin is shaved clean? My chemicals dripped down and did that!

These chemicals are called antibiotics. When you're sick, they can kill the bad bacteria inside your body so you get better. I'm just a fuzzy, gray mold, but you may owe your good health to me.

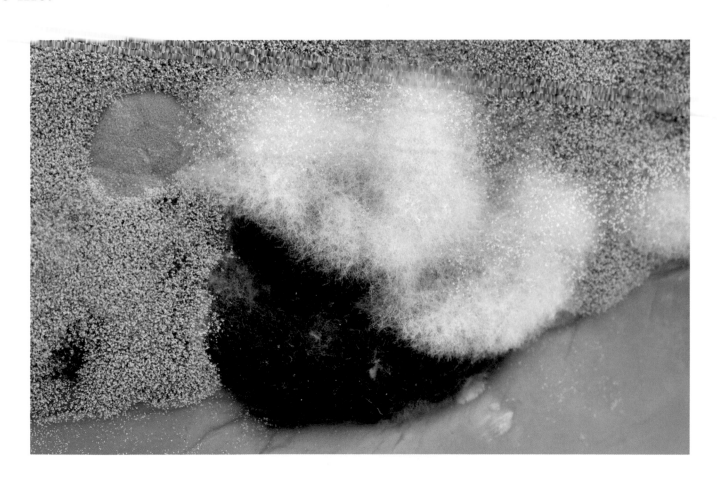

Am I still a pumpkin? My top is collapsing, and my skin is a mess of molds. They grow all over each other and right through me, eating my flesh from the outside-in and from the inside-out! Not even winter snows and low temperatures have slowed them down because most of the fungi that love pumpkins thrive in cold weather. How did I get so unlucky?

Don't call me a lowly earthworm. The only thing low about me is my place on the ground. The work I do is high and mighty. Dead leaves, flowers, fruit, and animal carcasses are healthy food to me! When I eat a hunk of rotten pumpkin, its nutrients go into my mouth and many go out the other end. Now they are part of the soil. They will nourish growing plants, including new pumpkins! See, I'm not lowly at all.

I am everywhere – in the air, in the soil, in your body and on this pumpkin. I am a single cell, which means I'm too small for you to see without a microscope. When millions like me cover a piece of fruit, you'll notice a whitish film. That's me, yeast.

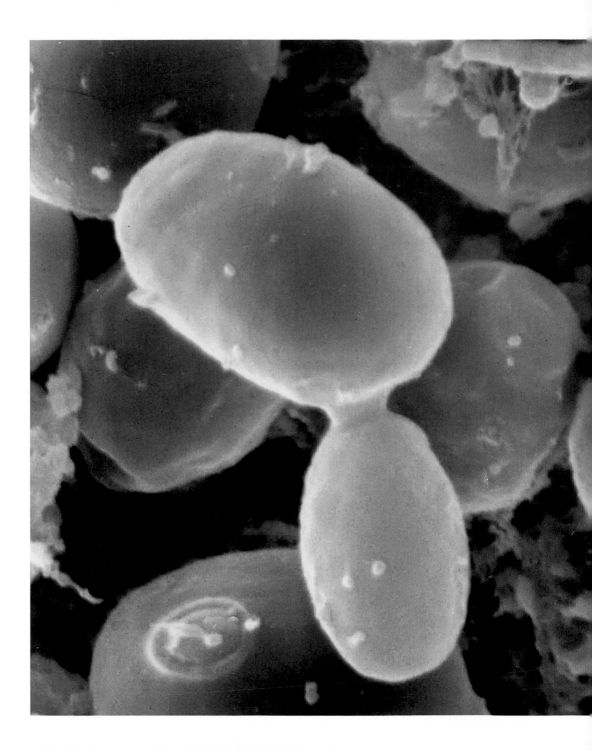

Some kinds of yeast help bread dough rise. Other kinds turn grape juice into wine and cocoa beans into chocolate. We all digest sugar and release carbon dioxide along with alcohol. This is called fermentation. When you bake bread, the alcohol burns off but the gas bubbles get trapped. They expand from the heat and stretch the dough to make it soft and puffy.

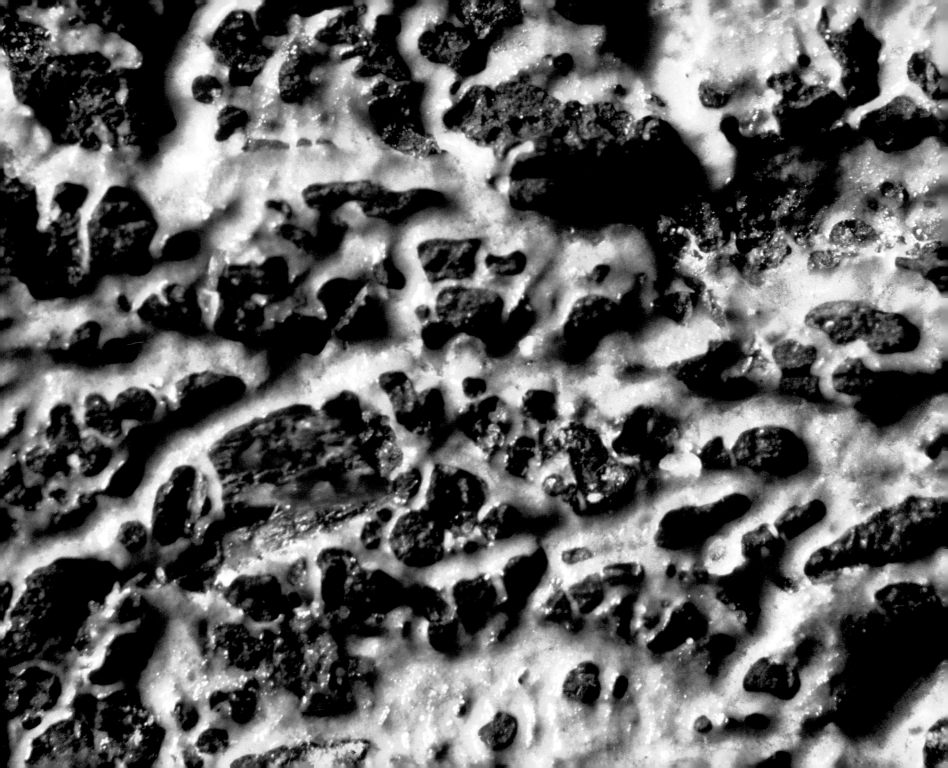

Of all the strange things growing on this pumpkin, I am the strangest. I am a slime mold. I started as a single cell, tumbling through the soil. Every once in a while I divided in half so there were two of "me." Soon there were lots and lots of us. Then we did the oddest thing: we joined to become one living creature that spread out in squiggly yellow arms connected like a net. The net, called a "plasmodium," began to move.

As a plasmodium, I oozed around for a while, then I landed on this pumpkin stem and changed shape again. I sent up stalks with spore cases that look like tiny red balloons. Gazillions of spores will grow in them, then they'll fly away in the wind, and the slime mold cycle will begin anew. Sounds like an alien life-form, doesn't it?

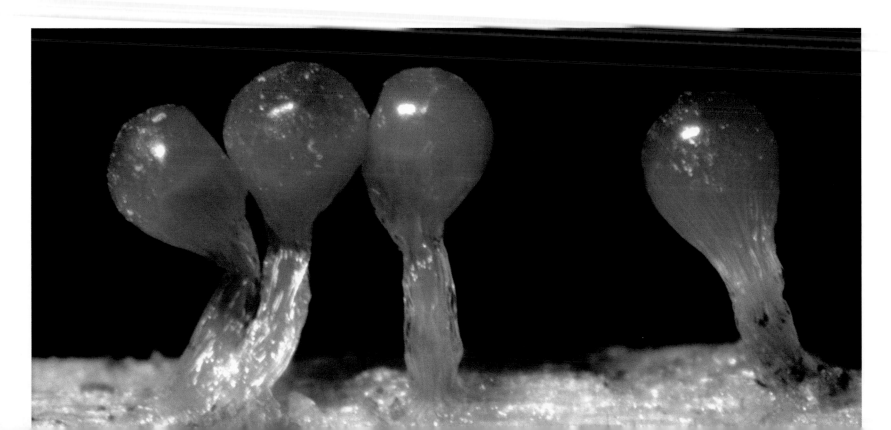

My pumpkin days are done. My pumpkin pride is gone. My pumpkin future? None. I'm a smelly rotten mess spilling my seeds on the garden soil. Am I good for anything now?

I think of myself as a mother, the mother of all that grows on the land. I give seeds the molecules of nourishment they need. And what happens to these molecules when the plants die? They return to me.

But I cannot pluck these molecules from dead plants as a hand picks fruit. They must be released by decomposers – the molds and rots, the earthworms and sowbugs, the many fungi, yeast, and bacteria. Even flies, birds, squirrels, mice, and slugs do their part. With decomposers working, working, working non-stop, the earth is a fruitful place.

There were hundreds of seeds like me, slippery and moist, connected by a stringy web. One day a hand reached inside and scooped out most of us. That hand missed me. Through bright, sunny days and long, stormy nights, I sat inside the pumpkin.

The animals came, the molds grew, the pumpkin collapsed into a heap of goo. . . and I waited. The goo seeped into the soil, enriching it with nutrients . . . and I waited. I nestled in pumpkin-soil, warming from the sun's energy, swelling with spring rains, pushing roots downward and stem upward. If all goes well, my flowers will form fruit.
My fruits will ripen.

Maybe one of them will be your next Jack O'Lantern.
Maybe it will have a glory day of its own.

GLOSSARY

bacterium (plural **bacteria**) Tiny, single-celled living things that are not plants, animals or fungi, but in a category by themselves. Bacteria are known for causing diseases but many kinds are harmless or even helpful. (For example, humans and many other animals need bacteria in their guts to digest food.)

decompose Literally, to "take apart." **Decomposers** are organisms that break down dead things or organic matter and recycle their nutrients so they can be used again by other organisms. The process is called decomposition.

fungus (plural **fungi**) A type of living thing that is neither a plant nor an animal. Unlike plants, fungi do not make their own food. They feed off of plants, animals, or organic matter (such as a pumpkin, which is the fruit of a plant). Molds, mildews, and yeasts are types of fungi. Mushrooms are the spore-producing, fruiting bodies of some fungi.

mold A type of fungus found in almost all environments that grow on and inside their food (often plant matter) by producing slender filaments, called hyphae. The hyphae form an interconnected network called a mycelium. Molds reproduce through **spores** which they produce in small bodies that may appear fuzzy or dusty. Molds require moisture to grow.

penicillin An drug originally made from the mold Penicillium which was observed in 1929 by a British doctor, Alexander Fleming, to prevent the growth of nearby bacteria. Because it works against living cells, it is called an "antibiotic" drug. Word of this "miracle drug" and its germ-killing power spread worldwide, and penicillin has been extracted from many species of Penicillum. A moldy cantaloupe in Illinois was found to have the most potent form. Penicillin continues to save lives, although related drugs are more effective for treating some infections. Some of the varieties are made synthetically.

rot (verb) To decompose or break down dead organic matter. (noun) A kind of mold or other fungus that decomposes plants.

spore The tiny (usually single-celled) reproductive body of fungi, algae, and some non-flowering plants that can grow into new organisms. Unlike seeds, which are usually larger and contain food to help the tiny plant inside get started, spores are produced without sexual fusion of male and female cells.

CLASSROOOM INVESTIGATIONS

The decomposition of a pumpkin presents many opportunities for students to **ask questions, make predictions (or formulate hypotheses), make observations, and draw conclusions.** They can also engage in the final step of the scientific method, which is to **publish** (or write about) the results of their experiments.

Scientists find ways to quantify their observations, meaning they make measurements and collect data. Instead of saying, "Pumpkin A looks more rotten than Pumpkin B," they record the approximate percentage of each pumpkin's surface area covered with decomposers, the number of different decomposers, or the time it has taken to completely decompose. Students can decide for themselves how they will record their observations.

Here are three questions students might ask in order to generate an experiment:

Does temperature affect decomposition?
Two similar pumpkins can be placed in environments at different temperatures. What happens?

Does carving a pumpkin change what grows on it or how fast it decomposes?
One pumpkin can be carved and a similar one left whole. The progress of decomposition for each can be recorded. A time interval for observations (daily, every other day, weekly, monthly, etc.) should be decided upon in advance. Students can compare how much and how quickly decomposition occurs on the pumpkins. Alternatively, they can observe the diversity of decomposers in the two situations. If there is a difference, they can speculate on the reasons.

Does the decomposition process change when animals are involved?
Think of a way to exclude creatures over a certain size from visiting one pumpkin, while leaving another pumpkin open to all visitors. But also think about whether the means of excluding animals changes the pumpkin's environment in other ways. For example, if a pumpkin is put in a tight metal box, small animals would be excluded but other factors would also be different. The pumpkin would be in the dark. The humidity inside the box might be higher than outside the box. In scientific experiments, it is best to change only one factor, or variable, at a time.